# LEGENDARY PHOENIXES

FANTASY CREATURES

Gareth Stevens PUBLISHING

HOT TOPICS

BY BENJAMIN PROUDFIT

Please visit our website, www.garethstevens.com. For a free color catalog of all our high-quality books, call toll free 1-800-542-2595 or fax 1-877-542-2596.

**Library of Congress Cataloging-in-Publication Data**
Names: Proudfit, Benjamin author
Title: Legendary phoenixes / Benjamin Proudfit.
Description: Buffalo, NY : Gareth Stevens Publishing, [2026] | Series: Fantasy creatures | Includes index.
Identifiers: LCCN 2025021091 (print) | LCCN 2025021092 (ebook) | ISBN 9781482475289 (library binding) | ISBN 9781482475272 (paperback) | ISBN 9781482475296 (ebook)
Subjects: LCSH: Phoenix (Mythical bird) | Phoenix (Mythical bird) in literature
Classification: LCC GR830.P4 P76 2026 (print) | LCC GR830.P4 (ebook) | DDC 398.24/54–dc23/eng/20250626
LC record available at https://lccn.loc.gov/2025021091
LC ebook record available at https://lccn.loc.gov/2025021092

Published in 2026 by
Gareth Stevens Publishing
2544 Clinton Street
Buffalo, NY 14224



Designer: Leslie Taylor
Editor: Kristen Nelson

Photo credits: Cover, 5, 7, 19 (phoenix) Shutterstock AI Generator/Shutterstock.com; cover and series art (neon circle) Ikrill/Shutterstock.com, (rough frame) TarnishArt/Shutterstock.com, (splotchy background) TiffanyShanks/Shutterstock.com; p. 9 (egyptian writing) Abrilla/Shutterstock.com, (inset phoenix) Declan Hillman/Shutterstock.com; p. 11 Anonymous artist, 17th cent. or 18th cent. Mughal India./File:NLM MS P 2-fol187b-anqa.jpg_commons.wikimedia.org; p. 13 griannan/Flickr.com; p. 15 Bernard Gagnon/File:Longshan Temple - Fenghuang.jpg_commons.wikimedia.org; p. 21 Ellianne/Shutterstock.com; p. 23 Futuras Fotos/Alamy.com; p. 25 (background) amgun/Shutterstock.com, (helmet) Sarunyu L/Shutterstock.com; p. 27 Karen Roe/Flickr.com; p. 29 (phone) MemoryMan/Shutterstock.com, (card) Simbert Brause/Shutterstock.com; p. 30 (band) Raph_PH/Flickr.com; (AZ) Brent Coulter/Shutterstock.com, (flag) rarrarorro/Shutterstock.com, (opera house) Yuri Turkov/Shutterstock.com, (mascot) Royalbroil/File:UWGBMascot2010.jpg_commons.wikimedia.org.



Printed in China

CPSIA compliance information: Batch #QWGS26: For further information contact Gareth Stevens, at 1-800-542-2595.

# CONTENTS

# Look to the Sky

Something that sets **fantasy** stories apart are the many creatures that live in these worlds. They're often magical and do impossible things. Phoenixes are **mythical** birds you may know from books or movies. They certainly *spark* the imagination!

## IMAGINE THAT!

THE SPELLING OF PHOENIX DOESN'T MATCH HOW YOU SAY IT: "FEE-NICKS."

# Ancient Myth

Myths of the phoenix date back to **ancient** Egypt. It was a sacred, or holy, bird for this **culture**. The story goes that the phoenix came to a certain place every 500 years. There, it would burn up—and then rise from its own ashes!

## IMAGINE THAT!

THE PHOENIX WAS SAID TO LIVE A VERY, VERY LONG TIME. ONLY ONE WAS ALIVE AT A TIME.

In Egyptian myths, the phoenix was large and had beautiful red and gold feathers. Before its death, it built a nest and then set it on fire. It then burned up for good. A new phoenix was born from the flames of the nest.

## IMAGINE THAT!

PHOENIXES **SYMBOLIZED** IMMORTALITY IN ANCIENT EGYPT AS WELL AS ANCIENT GREECE. IMMORTALITY MEANS LIVING FOREVER.

# Other Mythical Birds

Other cultures have mythical birds with some power. Some are more similar to the phoenix than others. Stories from Islam tell of a phoenix-like bird called *anqā*. It was said to hold a lot of wisdom, and seeing it meant big changes were on the way.

**IMAGINE THAT!**

ISLAM IS THE FAITH FOLLOWED BY MUSLIMS. THEY BELIEVE IN ONE GOD CALLED ALLAH AND A **PROPHET** CALLED MUHAMMAD.

## ANQĀ

Hindu mythology tells of a bird called Garuda. The god Vishnu rode on him, and he is sometimes a symbol of Vishnu. Garuda was emerald green and had golden wings. It had features of a bird called a kite and an eagle.

## IMAGINE THAT!

GARUDA IS SAID TO HAVE GIVEN SNAKES THE ABILITY TO SHED, OR LOSE, THEIR SKINS.

GARUDA

# The Caladrius

Roman mythology tells of the Caladrius, an all-white, mythical bird that knows if someone will die. It can also take sickness from a person. Then, it flies to the sun where the illness can burn up. The person is then made well!

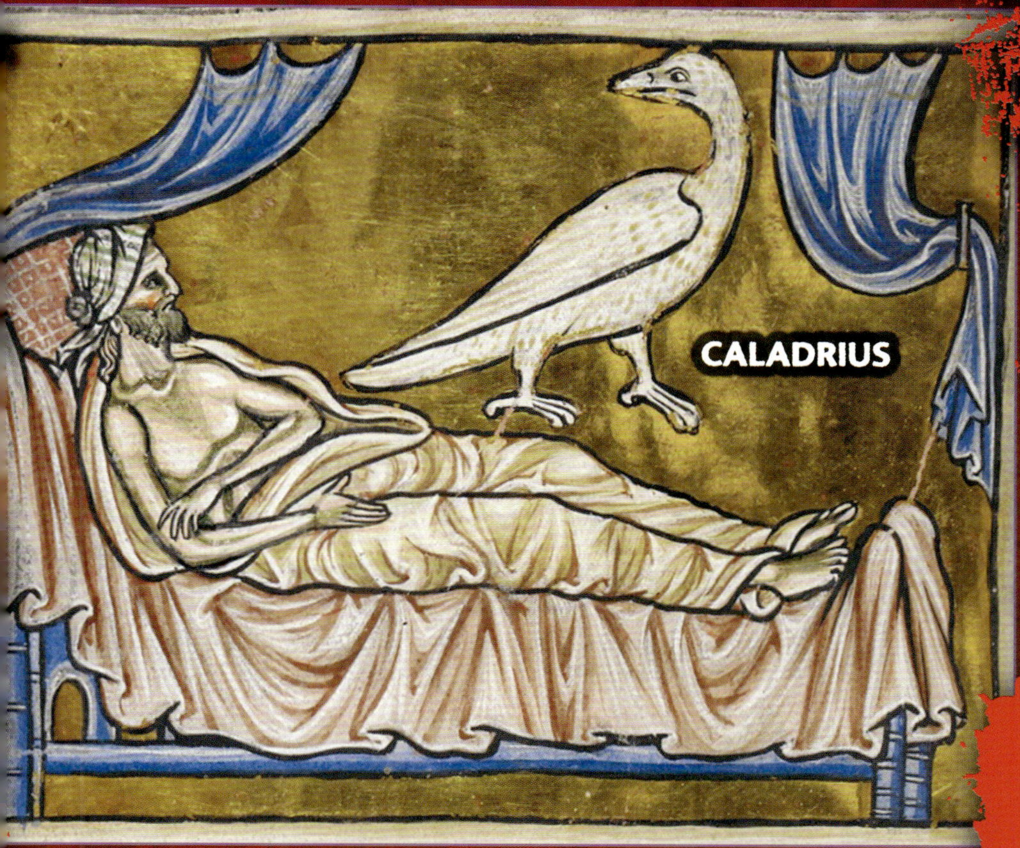


## IMAGINE THAT!

THE CALADRIUS SOMETIMES STANDS FOR JESUS CHRIST, THE CENTRAL FIGURE OF CHRISTIANITY THAT CHRISTIANS BELIEVE DIED FOR THEIR SINS.

# The Chinese Phoenix

Chinese culture has a mythical bird too. It's called the Fenghuang. It symbolizes balance as well as the sky, moon, wind, earth, and planets. While it doesn't burn to be reborn, like the phoenix, the Fenghuang is said to be immortal.

## IMAGINE THAT!

ANOTHER MYTHICAL BIRD COMES FROM THE FENGHUANG IN CHINESE MYTHOLOGY—THE VERMILLION BIRD.

FENGHUANG

# Shakespeare

We know the phoenix remained part of culture because English writer William Shakespeare wrote about it! He wrote the **poem** "The Phoenix and the Turtle," which came out in 1601. He also includes a phoenix in Sonnet 19, another poem.

## IMAGINE THAT!

SHAKESPEARE'S WORKS HAVE OTHER FANTASY CREATURES IN THEM, INCLUDING WITCHES. HIS PLAY *A MIDSUMMER NIGHT'S DREAM* HAS FAIRIES!

DRAWING OF A SCENE FROM *A MIDSUMMER NIGHT'S DREAM*

# Phoenixes in Pop Culture

Phoenixes have long been used in books, movies, and games. In the 1950s, C. S. Lewis wrote about the mythical bird in the popular series *The Chronicles of Narnia*. The series also features dwarves, a dragon, and other creatures from mythology.

## IMAGINE THAT!

IN THE 2005 MOVIE OF LEWIS'S *THE LION, THE WITCH, AND THE WARDROBE*, A PHOENIX APPEARS TO AID THE HEROES IN FIGHTING THE WHITE WITCH, QUEEN JADIS.

In 1976, *X-Men* comic book fans met Phoenix for the first time. She was Jean Grey, also known as Marvel Girl, powered by the **cosmic** Phoenix Force. When using the Phoenix Force, Grey looks like she is surrounded by a flaming bird!

## IMAGINE THAT!

WHEN GREY DIES, SHE BECOMES ONE WITH THE PHOENIX FORCE.

X-MEN
MARVEL COMICS GROUP
APPROVED BY THE COMICS CODE AUTHORITY
30¢
101
OCT
02461
THE ALL-NEW, ALL-DIFFERENT
X-MEN
IN THE MUTANT HEROES' HOUR OF MAXIMUM PERIL...
ENTER: THE PHOENIX!
COCKRUM

The symbol of the heroes' Rebel Alliance in the *Star Wars* movies is sometimes called the Starbird. It's a phoenix rising from the ashes. It's meant to show how the Alliance will bring about a new government after taking down the evil Empire.

## IMAGINE THAT!

THE FIRST *STAR WARS* MOVIE CAME OUT IN 1977. MANY MOVIES AND SHOWS HAVE COME OUT SINCE, WITH MORE PLANNED TO COME.

STARBIRD

A phoenix plays a big role in the *Harry Potter* series. Fawkes the phoenix is the companion of the important wizard Albus Dumbledore. Fawkes burns up and is reborn right in front of Harry Potter in one of the books!

**IMAGINE THAT!**

FAWKES'S TEARS CAN HEAL.

Phoenixes have been featured in many video games too, including *Final Fantasy, Paper Mario,* and *Sonic*. The Pokémon Ho-Oh is based on a phoenix too! Who knew a story of a bird from ancient history could be so cool?

**IMAGINE THAT!**

**THE CARD GAME MAGIC: THE GATHERING HAS FEATURED MORE THAN 30 DIFFERENT PHOENIX CARDS!**

POKÉMON GO GAME

HO-OH CARD

**PHOENIX**
rock band from France

**PHOENIX**
Arizona's capital city

San Francisco, CA city flag

# Phoenixes All Around

**LA FENICE**

opera house in Venice, Italy, that has burned down twice and been rebuilt both times

**COLLEGE SPORTS TEAM MASCOTS**

Cumberland University

Elon University

Wilson College

University of Wisconson Green Bay

**PHLASH THE PHOENIX**

# FOR MORE INFORMATION

## BOOKS

Munsey, Lizzie, et al. *Supernatural Creatures: Mythical and Sacred Creatures from Around the World.* New York, NY: DK, 2024.

Nardo, Don. *Creatures and Beasts in World Mythology.* San Diego, CA: ReferencePoint Press, Inc., 2025.

## WEBSITES

**Fantasy Books for Kids**
*https://www.commonsensemedia.org/lists/fantasy-books-for-kids*
Find lots of great fantasy books for kids here.

**Fantasy Movies for Kids**
*https://www.commonsensemedia.org/lists/best-fantasy-movies*
Find your next favorite fantasy movie here!

# GLOSSARY

**ancient:** Very old.

**cosmic:** Having to do with the universe outside of Earth.

**culture:** The beliefs and ways of life of a group of people.

**fantasy:** Having to do with imaginative stories that feature impossible events and characters.

**mascot:** An animal or character adopted by a school team to bring luck and cheer.

**mythical:** Having to do with myths, which are stories that were told by a people to explain a practice, belief, or natural event.

**poem:** A piece of writing in verse that may tell a story.

**prophet:** Someone with special insight granted from a god or gods.

**symbolize:** To stand for. A symbol is a picture, shape, or object that stands for something else.

# INDEX